Keeping in Place

poems by

Mary Ricketson

Finishing Line Press
Georgetown, Kentucky

Keeping in Place

Copyright © 2021 by Mary Ricketson
ISBN 978-1-64662-549-9 First Edition
All rights reserved under International and Pan-American Copyright Conventions. No part of this book may be reproduced in any manner whatsoever without written permission from the publisher, except in the case of brief quotations embodied in critical articles and reviews.

ACKNOWLEDGMENTS

"Sick When COVID went Viral," *Pendemic* (online journal for pandemic poems based in Armagh Ireland, http://pendemic.ie) 5-25-20

"How to Get Happy," *Enjoy the Holidays,* a poetry and prose anthology by Old Mountain Press, October 2020

Publisher: Leah Huete de Maines
Editor: Christen Kincaid
Cover Art: R. Alex Peers
Author Photo: Lorinda Baker
Cover Design: Elizabeth Maines McCleavy

Order online: www.finishinglinepress.com
also available on amazon.com

Author inquiries and mail orders:
Finishing Line Press
PO Box 1626
Georgetown, Kentucky 40324
USA

Table of Contents

Sacred 1

Keeping in Place 3

The Trouble with Home 4

In the Frightened World of Corona 5

Power of Pandemic 6

Sick when COVID went Viral 7

Desire 9

Attacked by a Chicken While Quarantined Away
    from Coronavirus 10

Visits in Times of Social Distance 11

Pandemic Pandemonium 12

Beauty for Social Distance 13

Not Last Year 14

Hello it's Simple 15

Dig that Dirt 16

My Contemplation 18

Cobbled in Weird 19

Wishing on a Wing 20

Magic Place 21

How to Get Happy 22

Unbroken 23

Mountain at Dawn 24

Home in the Woods 25

COVID 19 in the Mild 26

For Lee

Sacred

After the long solitude
I will teach poetry
in quiet places,
share the lures of listen and see.

Count on wisdom of walnuts,
their rugged bark of protection,
deep brown dye for basket weave,
nutmeats, food worthy of the gods.

I am the Solomon seal,
undaunted by storms
constant along the woodland trail,
flowers of pearl droplets
seen by bend, kneel into dirt.

Look, the laurel in the mountains,
how it blooms like pink
patchwork quilt rounds sewn
together with swatches of green
and mists of yellow sun
marbled with rain
and stunned by storm.

Steep mountain sides of calico
blooms, delicate pale pink, preside
where nature winds and twists,
defies domestication by trail.

Easy glimpses startle a pause,
give peace that seeps in, soft
like a memory, slow dancing
with someone you love.

Bystanders stare in passion,
anointed by nature, beauty unexpected.
After corona, beauty will teach its ways
in words of silence, words of listen.

Keeping in Place

Purple phlox blooms on the south creek bank in April.
Again my pulse sings at first sight, same as every year.
You could say those flowers keep me here.
You could say it was the sun, wind, clouds,
birds, or the ever flowing creek.
None of that would be wrong.

Mention the moon, its graceful rise
over the mountain, how it keeps its own pace,
crosses the sky of its own will, till trees
to the west hide its body, whether full
or only the silver sliver.
Mention the moon, and you will not be wrong.

Dogwood blooms in April, after weeping cherries
cry their fill from full flower to drop.
Sometimes the purple blooms of redbud
offset the pristine white of dogwood crosses.
When the full pink moon shines tonight,
you will see what I mean, and we will not be wrong.

The Trouble with Home

I almost told you the stink bugs are not so bad
now that it is March and I was gone two weeks
and they had no one to bother,
but then one landed on the pillow next to me
as I woke early in the morning,
not the lover I've been looking for.

That scaly grey armor atop spindly legs,
buzzing sound when it spins and plops
unwanted where least expected,
is good for nothing but scare and spite.
If this is not the uninvited guest,
I'd hate to think of who'd be worse.

These weeks away, I thought I'd come
home to things as I left them,
but change weaves its own way.
A virus worse than stink bugs presides.
Now the peepers call, turn season to spring,
no matter the fates uninvited.

In the Frightened World of Corona

One crow flies, caws, its common wing spread
the marvel of my morning.

One old bicycle body has rusted forever inside
the arms of a beech tree on the corner.

Can that tree hold our health in this time of corona?
Can that crow carry messages farm to farm?

And what does the sky have in mind for our world today?

Power of Pandemic

An unseen world
alters me, shifts and shakes
these weeks and weeks
I stay at home.

One pileated woodpecker
darts down the air, dares
me catch a glimpse of his beauty
black and red, before he's gone.

One bored cow, pastured alone
to fatten, chews on a cardboard box,
stands all day behind two strands
of electric fence.

Now bluebird pairs fly free,
follow ploy, paths of instinct.
Well out of sight a female sits,
nests her young, and waits.

Away from here,
where the groceries are,
six feet bless the distance
between me and you.

I count the days
since I've been touched.

Sick when COVID went Viral

That day in March, trees said spring is just around the corner.
Daffodils bloomed. I hated to make the phone call.

Trip alone to urgent care, set up by health department nurse:
see to the bad cough, worse day by day, trouble breathing,
time to worry, find help quick.

Park in back, in sight of the side door. Wait. Staff will meet you.
What car are you driving? What time will you get there?

Almost dark that night in March, I backed into a parking spot, watched
   the door.
Full PPE, a person spoke from behind layers of mask and helmet:
Bring only car key and *billfold*. Into exam room, vitals and tests:
You don't have the flu. You do have strep throat. We can't test for Covid 19,
there's a shortage. Hospital? I preferred not.

I heard the phone call to another doc: *Just making sure,*
don't think we need inpatient admission. What do you think?
I held my breath. *No, I don't think she needs the ventilator.*

Antibiotic. First dose now. *You can go home. Stay alone. You're
   quarantined,*
in case you have coronavirus. Send a neighbor to a drug store tomorrow
for the rest of your antibiotic. Don't go yourself, not even the drive through
   window.
If you have trouble breathing tonight, don't wait for it to get worse. Call 911.
Tell them you are quarantined, so paramedics can prep, full PPE.

Stars came out. I made it home. Nurse and PA daily phone calls were
   my lifeline
till wellness alone won me over. Back to work. Two days later, work
   from home, risk

seems all too much. One week later: *You were near someone exposed to the virus.*
Come get tested, quarantine alone till results. One week later: *Negative* was one happy word.

Desire

Look deep down in the shallow creek,
bottom of a narrow gorge.
Watch your step. Don't fall in.
See the treasure, golden oval-fan petals,
delicate and pristine,
irises atop long green pointed spears
grace the space,
three beauties in the afternoon sun.

Should I make a wish?
Sure these floral royals, hidden treasures
self-planted from some exotic paradise,
can grant my desire. If I am good.

**Attacked by a Chicken While Quarantined Away
from Coronavirus**

My normal walk, way out in the country,
trots me along a dirt driveway, on to a narrow paved road
where houses stand an acre or more apart, room
for horses, mules, and trout streams, presided by regal presence
of a red tailed hawk, black crows and all colors of song birds.

A brown calf moos every morning to me, runs along his side
of a two row barb wire fence, keeps pace with me.
Friends for months now, I look forward to his company.
Next to him, white leghorn chickens sometimes run free.

One big hen, clean white offset by red comb and waddle,
moseyed across the road, never said why, slammed
right into my thigh like serious business,
and pecked me with her beak.

Why did the chicken cross the road?

Visits in Times of Social Distance

Past the barn and two field mules,
my walk takes me near both neighbors,
on down by the abandoned house
where the beech tree reigns,
alongside my mailbox
left by the cornfield, then right.

Before the rugged Rose Creek bridge,
I cross the road to a pasture,
visit with a bull calf who eats grass,
clangs a yellow bell of a necktie.

He was a tiny calf all those months ago,
young enough for me to ooh and aah
without embarrassing him.
Now I compliment him, so grown up,
strong and sturdy, dignified bright sheen
to his mahogany brown coat.

I walk on to the bridge where creek flow
runs deep, holds my secret hopes and dreams,
linger a long moment like always, then walk back
by the pasture and the calf, not really mine.

He trots toward me most every time now,
looks me in the eye, close up, listens to me talk,
like he knows I'm falling in love
even though a two strand barb wire
always separates us, even though I know
his time in the pasture is short.

Pandemic Pandemonium

Powerful corona rules a world
where creeks always flow, grass still grows
and no one knows which breath will kill.

Preston the postal clerk handed me
someone's receipt, not my package,
then we laughed, got it right.

Jazzie, my Monday appointment,
left her cell phone unattended,
said it seemed to be Sunday all day long.
We both laughed, rescheduled next day.

I called the wrong person on Wednesday,
embarrassed myself,
relieved when laughter wrapped us both.

Hilarious in our masks and gloves,
whatever safety demands, a world steps
in stride, sports smiles unseen, imagined
from roots deep in human tenacity.

Harley the grocer steps back to make social
distance from me, a new kind of hello.
Always, dizzy inane un-excusables fill loopholes,
bump and grind, buy all the toilet paper,
none to be found now.

Beauty for Social Distance

Star of Bethlehem,
flower beauty,
six soft white petals
in perfect star open bright,
close every night.

Spotted at the edge
of a well-trod path,
white sparkles
shine, sit above dirt,
grime and stone.

Friendly to the eye,
pure poison in all parts,
this floret buds for our time,
more an apple of Eden
than treasure of Magi.

Keep six feet away.
Do not touch.

Not Last Year

This world looks different
out my left eye than my right.
Town is partly open, partly not.
Get a massage, see a movie,
even grab a beer, but don't expect
to go inside the bank lobby
or an office or a school.

Now the world lives by social media,
zoom, cameras and microphones,
in place of human touch.
I walk this country road,
watch a cow stare at me from his pasture.
I speak to him as though he is human.

Hello It's Simple

Hello from here, I told the mule.
Too muddy to get up close to the fence,
first rays of sun shine bright as gold.
Dogs keep me on schedule,
long strides down path, our usual walk.

Blue sky seems such a smile
after a hard siege of weather.
Loose rocks slide and tumble,
bumble astray in the graveled bed.
What else will these shoes bear?

Now the cow runs a playful jig
across the pasture to meet me.
Chickens decline to attack me today.
Black cap chickadees and birds
I have not named dart in cheerful flight.

In the hands of this pandemic,
trying not to panic much,
animals my best friends
as if it were normal,
I wonder about the change in me.

If I settle, learn new levels of content
past first lonely, past the longings,
what will remain of the life I once knew?

Dig that Dirt

Big ass work is what it takes.
Beat those corona blues,
get the rhythm right.

Become the soil,
take nurture. Surrender
to spade, place, air, and rain.
Allow dirt to kindle
fires of change.
Only basics visible,
future reveals, layer by layer
till a bed of loose rich dirt,
sieved and softened, wakes
to asparagus roots.
Plant with care.

On the day I think
I may never thrive again,
Covid 19 everywhere,
not a drop of hope
except one dogwood flower,
in a moment
that single redbird calls,
speaks the sounds of life.

Bless Nature, truly Mother,
who pets my head with her breeze,
knows what I need,
feeds me views of trees,
sends dogwoods in flower,
maples leafed out new,
rain on lettuce greens and broccoli,
birds to call in the morning.

A pretty bad rough patch
calls for big ass work:
Shovel, trowel, and rake.
Sweat your fear and worry into soil.
Clean out your stress filled mind.
Empty all and win with a big, full heart
to beat the blues.

My Contemplation

In the time of weather changes,
wild, crazy and unexpected,
down past all the white pines,
sun shines in the quiet place.

A fringe tree blooms white there
after wild cherries, before sourwood,
and when the blackberries blossom,
white flowers all.

White clover and daisies welcome
stillness while the air is cool.
Walking with my old white coat
clutched tight, I beg the sun, *Come strong*.

Then the wind stirs wild again,
a red and white pileated woodpecker screeches
Good morning, swoops around the open cove
then flies back into the deep dense woods.

Farther down path, a walnut shows green leaf,
dressed for summer in a world we won't know
anymore as normal. Humans scratch up ingenious
ways to live through pandemic fear and loss

of unknown guise, wile and duration.
Beyond the bend where chickens and horses live,
a rusty TV antenna and two unused clothes lines
at the empty house speak of life once understood.

Walking home, past red farm implements,
pitch forks in place by shovels and pic axes,
where even gravel looks bright against darkest dirt,
one white iris sings her promise of hope.

Cobbled in Weird

It takes so much shoe these days
to hold me up and keep me going.
My brown brogans fit like a glove,
brave the arch that fell away,
tie the ankle that loves near naked bone.
Imagination slides between the laces.

Bind the toes, colored nails socked
beyond sight, beyond avail.
Laugh no more at memories of Granny shoes,
frightful enigma of my childhood,
I'll never wear any shoe like that,
I mentored my young self.

Hike on, dear feet, meta-morph
into whatever age may come.
Pandemic turns eye to another beauty,
sutures half-lives to each other
in the brilliant blur of reality
where sunshine meets the rain.

Wishing on a Wing

A pair of blue birds plays house,
nest ready to begin a second family
in the new moon of May.

See that rusty red male breast,
perfect blue back as he turns
on the iron arch near his domain
in the old azalea bush.

Now the female swaps places.
Imagine wishes and plans, raise
a family from soft blue eggs
to wings of feather and flight.

Red cardinal flits in a nearby bush.
Sunshine, so magical its power
in rain and dark thunder storms,
will peek through clouds today.

Unknown forces insist to visit,
weave ways into the garden
where life plants itself,
chance what takes root or not.

The grey tufted titmouse at the feeder,
crested feathers flitting in the wind,
seems to understand this urgent time
where life wishes for its own breath,
and death waits on a wing.

Magic Place

Year by year those ferns speak
traditions of simple truth.
Trust in this forest soil,
its fertile, constant strains.

Blackberries bloom on briars,
tangles of flat leaves and stickers
right there on the edge of bad dirt
where no one would think to plant.
Beware the brash words, those who order
our world to their own expectations.
Winter bites back after warm,
has it's own way, brief frozen kiss,
then moves away, a sway of the wind.

Trillium and Solomon seal,
rare specimens of delight,
bloom by the rocky dirt path,
seen only by the slow of foot
and eyes enchanted by mystery,
lured by the mystic wave of a wand.
Pandemic kills, not safe to breathe
same air, human to human.
This land lives as giver of hope.

Up in the woods the ferns
grow lush and dense.
Secrets shelter in the soil,
share sage and mystic sensibilities
without language.

Low flyby of an indigo bunting
marks the silence of mystic ferns.

How to Get Happy

Wait for a breeze, hope that vine of honeysuckle
smells stronger, stirs a rush of fragrance in the air.

Will these climbing roses to open, dazzle the day with red.
Allow a prick of thorns when you grab a stem to keep.

Thank the gold and black buzzing pollinators in the garden.
Beware of attack. That territory is their own.

Taste the air when the tickling breeze finally bustles,
fresh as cold spring water from the source.

Push one honeysuckle blossom to your lips,
slip under the spell of sweet wishes and dreams.
Lazy away, charmed into a summer's day.

Unbroken

Outside, where truth resides,
this hemlock stump holds stories,
respite of strong summer shade,
green lace limbs a-sway in the breeze.

Down on Dockery Creek,
unharmed by the deadly *Wooly Adelgid*,
two healthy hemlocks stand
alive among oak, maple, and cherry.

The brown bull I call my own
is too grown, too proud to walk to the fence,
won't come close and greet me today,
keeps munching grass, plays hard to get.

I stand in full sun; listen to Rose Creek flow,
watch water dance under this bridge,
wonder what dies and what remains
when this pandemic is done.

I want to be one of those people
who say isolation was good for me in a way.
I want to thrive like those hemlocks
alive on the creek.

Mountain Dawn

Maybe I could be a mountain, serve eons
with ancient Appalachian oak and maple trees, grow
moss and mushrooms, trunk to crown, climb to the sky.

Moments of frivolity pump me up, make my arms
like blackbird wings, fly me high
past one crisp cumulous into the blue.

Look at the sun. Early rays reach down
into beech tree limbs. Soft crinkles shimmer
through thick summer green leaf.

First light on this poplar bark looks white.
I want to surround myself with trees
who make their own words.

Two tawny deer stand silent watch
where wide Cherry Cove meets the woods
still wise with night.

Mountainsides of wildflowers and fern wait
for the chosen hour of filtered sunshine.
Pink blush of rhododendron bloom in the bright.

Home in the Woods

Waiting for word, patience is a teacher.

Five deer, downfield at dawn, don't know coronavirus,
quarantine, social distance, or price of gas today.
Slow, they nibble grass at will, heads sway down,
white tails shine in the grey light just past night.
Then I watch their graceful romp to the tree flanked creek
for an after breakfast drink.

Later a flock of turkeys strut my field, scatter
as I start my daily walk.
I dodge puddles from last night's rain on the damp dirt path.
Dogs stomp down the middle.

Distracted by a memory, bruises and betrayals rise
like the dead coming out of their graves,
ask resolution and forgiveness again.

I move aside, sit quiet on a mossy rock, look east
where all days begin, sing with the birds, marvel
at pastels of early spring, then cup my hands, drink
from a pool of cool well water.

Blessings and benedictions performed,
a breeze today taps my shoulder.
Unfettered, no words or thoughts of pandemic,
I walk west and wait the time for sun to set.

COVID 19 in the Mild

Swirls of careful details, measure and bind,
give way to one bite, teeth thrust deep,
ignite a fear hiding in the blind.

Eastern hemlock struggles for life,
white speckles on green lace limbs.
Two-pronged poplar struggles with vines
of poison, nature's living threat.

My surprise phone call from a contact tracer,
then the test, and quarantine just in case,
then fever and symptoms, head cold gone wild,
exhaustion profound. The fear, the distance,
the go-it-alone and wish for flight.
Phone call of result: *Positive*, as the mend begins.
COVID 19 in the mild. No hospital. Future unknown.
Alone. Home. Thankful for life.
Waiting for my own fire to flame.

One crimson bloom shows on the Rose of Sharon bush.
Two dark hummingbirds dance among tall bee balm stalks.
Venus shines bright in the early night. From embers left to settle,
red orange flames rise to the fancies of life.

Many have died, many more to come.
Will to live soars to the farthest star
dares time to swerve, make way for wisdom and survival.

Mary Ricketson, Murphy NC, has been writing poetry 25 years. Inspired by nature and her work as a mental health counselor, her poetry has been published in Wild Goose Poetry Review, Future Cycle Press, Journal of *Kentucky Studies, Lights in the Mountains, Echoes Across the Blue Ridge, Red Fox Run, It's All Relative, Old Mountain Press, Whispers, Voices, Speckled Trout Review, The Lake, Your Daily Poem,* and her chapbook *I Hear the River Call my Name* (Finishing Line Press), and three full length poetry collections, *Hanging Dog Creek* (Future Cycle Press), and *Shade and Shelter* (Kelsay Books), *Mississippi: The Story of Luke and Marian* (Kelsay Books). She won first place in the 2011 Joyce Kilmer Memorial Forest 75th anniversary national poetry contest.

She writes a monthly column, "Woman to Woman," for *The Cherokee Scout* weekly newspaper in Cherokee County NC. She is a Licensed Clinical Mental Health Counselor and an organic blueberry farmer.

www.ingramcontent.com/pod-product-compliance
Lightning Source LLC
LaVergne TN
LVHW040118080426
835507LV00041B/1611